To The Newt,

EUANCA

EULINDA ANTONETTE CLARKE-AKALANNE

Much love

Empress Royále
Publishing

Antonette

[signature]

Disclaimer: The opinions expressed in EUANCA are those of the author and do not reflect the opinions of Empress Royále Publishing.

Edited by Theastarr Valerie

Cover design by Empress Royále Publishing

Cover image of Boabab Tree © **OpenClipart-Vectors**/pixabay.com

Picture © Eulinda Antonette Clarke-Akalanne

Empress Royále Publishing

Empressroyalepublishing@gmail.com

Facebook.com/empressroyalepublishing

Instagram.com/empressroyalepublishing

"Everything tells a story; let us help you tell your story to the world."

Euanca

EUANCA opens my heart in words

Sharing love, successes, and cares.

Much happiness and joy it bears.

Listen to the lessons

The content shares

The sadness, loss, and fears.

Listen to the beats of its heart.

To the rhythm and rhyme it imparts.

INTRODUCTION

My sister and I were brought up by strict Victorian standards and Roman Catholic dogmas. We were not allowed to bring home our school friends nor play with them outside of the school gates.

My mother decided who we could play with and these were her friends' children or those she approved of. She was in her mid-thirties when I was born, so the children of her friends were much older than I and they had no desire to play with me.

I was 4 years older than my sister who was usually my only playmate outside of school. She was mama's favorite child. As early as 3 years old, she realized her advantageous position in the family and she would often blame me for naughty things that she did.

Mama seemed to condone this behavior by not correcting her and I was often punished for things I did not do. My mother justified her punishment of me by using the trope *'you are the eldest'.*

My father worked for the British Merchant Navy and spent long periods away from home. Therefore, he had little influence in correcting this wrong. My punishments ranged from smacking to standing on one leg facing a wall with a book on my head.

I can still stand on one leg, sit and walk with a straight back today. Because of my experiences I resorted to the comfort of books and enjoyed the power of influence and mystery of words. It was therapeutic, providing me with a form of escapism, as well as imaginary playmates.

My love for poetry was influenced by my mother who was an avid storyteller and poetry performer. I started composing poems at the age of 7. The earliest one recorded in EUANCA is titled, *The Bumble Bee.* This tells of my fascination and childish curiosity with the natural world and my relationship with a humble bee.

The Windrush Generation and the Hostile Environment Bill is an epic poem which relates the trials and tribulations of Caribbean immigrants who, as British subjects, were invited to the United Kingdom to fill various job roles. It explains how, because of racism, many were rewarded with discrimination, prejudice, rejection and unjust treatment.

Every poem in the anthology is based on personal experiences, historical, political, and contemporary happenings, as well as the natural world.

The name of the book, *EUANCA*, is a combination of the first two letters of my first and middle names, and the first letter of each of my two surnames. EUANCA is diverse, is spans a variety of cultures and geographies.

The poems are intergenerational and provides something for everyone. EUANCA aims to educate, empower, motivate and inspire its readers.

DEDICATION

To my son William Vincent Clarke and my grandchildren: Grace May Antonette, Emmanuel, and Isaac Clarke.

ABOUT THE AUTHOR

Eulinda Antonette Clarke-Akalanne, fondly called Antonette, was born in Barbados where she spent her early youth. She is the widow of late barrister Chike Akalanne (LLB), and a mother and grandmother.

Among her many skills, Antonette acted in Shakespearian plays in school, starring as *Mark Anthony,* in 'Julius Caesar' and as *Juliet,* in 'Romeo and Juliet'.

In her school/church choir she sung soprano and was also a soloist. Antonette has written and performed poetry since her early childhood. Her epic poem, *The Windrush Generation and the Hostile Environment Bill,* was performed in the British Houses of Parliament in London on October 10, 2018.

From childhood, Antonette wanted to be a nun or an actress, but was dissuaded from both professions by her mother who believed that that the former was isolating and the latter a sinful occupation.

She opted to be a medical doctor, but family finances did not allow her to follow this path. At age 18, Antonette came to England to study to be a Registered General Nurse (RGN) in the National Health Service. After qualifying, she graduated and worked in other nursing disciplines as a Midwifery Sister, Senior Psychiatric Charge Nurse in a psychiatric Medium Secure Unit; Community Nursing Sister, and Health Visitor in Derbyshire, West Yorkshire, London and Somerset. She also studied for the Diploma in Social Work at the University of Bristol, and worked as a Social Worker in Bridgwater, Somerset, United Kingdom. Her desire to be a nun faded when she met a law student, who would later become her husband.

Now retired, Antonette is more active than ever. In 2018 she obtained a Bachelor of Arts degree in Anthropology at the University of Bristol in England and where she is now studying for a Master of Arts degree in Black

Humanities. She has a keen interest in Ancient African History and artifacts which she demonstrates in some of her poems.

Antonette's motto is: *learning is life long and life should be lived to its fullest potential for as long as possible.*

Antonette is engaged in composing and performing poems. She is also a short story writer, singer, and an actress. She acted in 'Breathing Fire', a Black women's Playback theatre company in Bristol and performed for Razana Afrika Company and acted in the film *'Fix Your Crown' as Queen Ndate Yala Mbodj* of the Waalo Kingdom. Antonette recently performed as *Girlie* in the film *'Hats'* for Fam Films Productions. This film is based on a true story.

ACKNOWLEDGEMENTS

I am indebted to my mother Erstine Matilda Clarke, aka Iris, for inspiring me in my creative journey. Her artistic vibrations flow through my veins and I am eternally thankful for this gift.

My deepest gratitude to my son, William Vincent Clarke, who faithfully listens to the recitations of my poems and offers constructive advice, words of encouragement and support. Thank you for being you. Son, I love you.

To my adopted daughter Nagina, thanks for appreciating my work, making inspiring and encouraging comments, and offering a listening ear.

A special thank you to Dorritt Okoye, who encouraged me to publish my poems. Without your persistent encouragement, EUANCA might have remained just a file on my computer.

Thanks to Judith Desbonne for   faithfully attending my performances and giving valuable feedback.

Tony Fernandez, thanks for inviting me to perform *The Windrush Generation and the Hostile Environment Bill,* at The Houses of Parliament. You helped to inform others about the plight of these people through this poem.

Gratitude to Miranda Rae for airing my poems on Ujima Radio Channel. You helped to spread my poems far and wide.
A massive thank you to Louise de Marchant and Gill Snow (project manager and assistant) of Global Fusion Music and Arts, for allowing me to perform my poetry and short stories monthly on GFMA's platform. This has increased my confidence in performing and has helped garner attention to my work.

Table of Contents

Poems by Eulinda Antonette Clarke-Akalanne

The Baobab Tree

In Queen's Park, Barbados,

not far from the sea,

stands an old, old,

Baobab tree.

    It is not a native of this island country.

From Africa, the seed floated   here
on the sea.

The Baobab has stood in this spot for over
1000 years.

    Beautiful white flowers the tree bears.

They are big

and exotic,

and grow out from the leaf axil.

                The flower buds

                only open at dusk.

Just like the night-blooming cereus,

but unlike the latter,

that has a beautiful aroma,

the Baobab flowers have a scented odor.

The flowers are

pollinated by nocturnal critters

such as moths, fire flies

and other night flitters.

In the morning, the flowers begin to wilt,

so to see the floral display,

keep a night vigil.

Its fruit are oval shaped,

large with hard shells,

which hang from the leaf axils like great
bells.

They are edible,

and very nutritious,

as well as exquisitely delicious.

The islanders know nothing about this...

They fear the fruit are poisonous.

The leaves contain micronutrients,
vitamins and proteins.

In Africa, the leaves are used in Kukan
soup and other meals.

90 feet tall, a girth of 8 feet,

the trunk is enormous.

Besides a medium sized house,

it is ginormous.

Few in the island reflect on this ancient
tree, except tourists

or returning nationals like me.

If the Baobab could speak about what it
could hear and see,

3

It will tell of first inhabitants' life history,

And when Europeans landed on the island
in the 17th century.

It would narrate the enslaved Africans
trials and their legacy,

and how Bussa, an enslaved African,
revolted against slavery,

but its secrets are kept locked in from you
and me,

In the solitude of silence,

in the trunk of the deciduous

Baobab tree.

BARBADOS

This small coral isle,

In the Caribbean-sea,

Birthed and nourished me.

Loss?

Two half-sisters that never met before,

were introduced to each other,

by their father.

One lived in Barbados, the other, Cape Town, South Africa.

From ages twelve to fourteen, they started corresponding.

At that time, there was no

internet nor texting.

They wrote to each other,

and shared their life stories with one another.

Linda, wrote about her school and
swimming in the sea.

Mona, her sister, told of life in District Six.

Linda wanted to become a doctor,

while Mona, hoped to be a dancer.

They exchanged photographs with one
another.

Linda resembled her mother,

and Mona, looked like their father.

They reminisce about things they had done,

and shared hopes and dreams for the years to
come.

Linda immigrated to England, was married,
has kids, more than one.

Mona stayed in her town and had Gasant,
her son.

The sisters hoped one day to meet,

but this was stopped by racist Apartheid.

Coloureds were forcibly removed to other
sites,

and D6 was razed to the ground and
reserved for Whites.

The sisters last corresponded in the
seventies.

And letters to Mona were returned stamped
'unknown'.

O where, o where had Mona gone?

Linda placed searches in the Argus
newspaper.

But no one responded to the adverts in this
media.

She enquired about her sister from South
Africans she had known,

asking, where the residents of D6 had gone.

This is like searching for a water drop in an
ocean,

because the respondents had no notion.

District 6 still lies fallow today,

but there are hopes that it will rise again
someday.

This is the legacy of the Apartheid regime,

A racist construct that was wicked and mean.

Destruction of D6 caused much suffering.

Destroying the residents' sense of belonging.

It treated people like cattle on auction,

Giving them little choice in their living location.

Linda is now an elder,

and desperately yearns to find her sister.

Could modern technology, mitigate this barrier?

Linda searched social media and found a fix,

related to 'Friends of District 6'.

Members were supportive, they cooperate,

and Cecile P. offered to investigate.

She learnt from Sylvie H that Mona was
alive and well,

The joy this has given is greater than one
can tell.

Cecile arranged a meeting on Zoom,

between the sisters, on the twenty seventh of
June.

Cecile, Sylvia H. and the D6 Team,

You are abundantly, thanked for fulfilling this dream.

Today is June, twenty-seven, two thousand twenty-one,

At eleven today the sisters, on Zoom, will meet again.

Linda is brimming with joy and expectation,

She wonders about their reaction,

after such a long separation,

when seeing and talking to each other on video/voice recording.

Ten to eleven the phone rings,

Linda is so ecstatic she almost sings.

Cecile calls to tell her that Mona passed.

On 9th April, eleven weeks ago, she breathed
her last.

Linda spirals from the top to the bottom

From joy and excitement to devastation.

She is broken hearted and sad,

but good has come out of the sorrow and the
bad.

Linda has made a new friend, Sylvia,

and she is now in contact with Gasant, her
nephew.

Awakening

Her hair grew in spirals, but she did not know it,

Because from childhood it was straightened every little bit.

This was first done with a metal comb heated on hot coals,

and moisturized with Vaseline oils.

Later electric combs were introduced.

This comb,

low,

medium,

or *high heat*

produced.

The girl dreaded the sessions of hair dressing,

Because of the risks of her scalp or ears burning.

Sometimes the dresser remembered a wrong she'd done,

and would take the opportunity to give her a burn,

reminding her of the peccadillo she had done.

The treated hair was glossy, black and straight,

but the girl had to avoid,

swimming in the lake,

because the hair would revert to spiral coils again.

Later in her life, chemical straighteners came in,

these were easy to apply and better than
hot combing,

Because straightened hair did not

re-curl after swimming,

and she didn't need an umbrella when it
was raining.

The girl now a woman, wears her hair
natural,

she knows the benefits of the coil and
spiral,

It's nature's way to keep the head cool in
hot climes,

There is no need to straighten the hair at
all,

Because there is fashion in the spiral and
coil.

The hair could be worn in cane rows,
twists or curls,

clean shaven, threaded or in locs,

Now, many pounds and pence the woman
is saving,

in hairdresser fees and boutique charging.

Plus, no damaged scalp or hair from
chemical straightening.

Summer Equinox

Equal day and night,

Is September twenty two,

Then nights get longer.

Nagina

Remember the workshop, Daughters of Africa,

when you came to speak to me, Nagina?

I was struck by your positive energy,

and the beautiful aura that emanated from thee.

It was long since I witnessed an aura so shining.

You glow with beauty without and within,

You have a harmony and peace about you,

in all the things that you say and do.

Nagina you are a special human being,

You are the reincarnation of a royal queen.

You are a caring and loving mother,

And a wonderful daughter.

You were sent to me, Nagina,

to be my non-biological daughter.

You are that daughter whom I can share my wisdom with.

I thank the Supreme Being for you,

you are a wonderful gift.

William

You are the love of my life, the apple of
my eye.

You have given me much happiness and
joy,

My precious son, my beloved boy.

You are an inspirational and wonderful
father,

As well as a caring and protective partner.

To me, you show love and loyalty,

showering me and others with your
generosity.

You are helpful, caring, kind and true,

empathetic through and through.

Son, I am so proud of you,

for the good that you have done and still do.

You are considerate and caring,

To the less fortunate you are giving.

Sometimes depriving yourself in sharing,

never asking for repay or a returning.

I remember the time when you were eleven,

and the driver struck a black bird in Devon,

You insisted that we stop and rescue it.

A beggar came to the table where we were dining,

She asked for cash and said she was starving,

You investigated and found out that normal meals were no good,

And that she could only consume gluten free food.

Leaving your hot dinner and your seat,

You made her a gluten free treat,

asking for nothing in return,

this was a lesson to learn.

The joy on her face was a delight to be seen,

it filled me with joy and I felt like a queen.

Son, you are a role model for us all.

Your heart is big and bold.

Son, you mean the world to me

I ask for cosmic blessings to be showered on thee.

Continue to beam your positive energy.

SUMMER SOLSTICE

Longest day of the year,

Is the twenty-first of June,

Night vanishes soon.

Women

We are daughters, aunts, and sisters,

friends, confidants, and mothers,

Queens and rulers of kingdoms,

Presidents and prime ministers of
nations,

creators of future generations,

Founts of love, hope and wisdom.

Energy and strength run through our
veins,

Successive generations we birth nourish
and sustain.

Women! Raise up your heads in pride,

Spread your wisdom wide.

Empower humanity with your vitality.

In female solidarity, let's reclaim our legacy.

Sail upon life's tide, spread your branches wide.

In unity soar upon life's tempestuous tide.

We are women, sisters, daughters,

Queens, mothers, and grandmothers.

We are the salt of the earth,

to generations of nations, we give birth.

AFRICA

O proud Africa,

The land of my ancestors,

Give us protection.

I am Afrikan

We were once called Blackamoors,

Ethiopians or Moors.

Then it was Coloureds,

Spades, wogs and Coons,

Niggers, Blacks or BAME's

Now 'People of colour' and Cultural Diversities.

We are labelled without our permission.

Given names that we have not chosen.

I must enlighten you anew,

I am Afrikan, through and through,

Regardless of the other bits that colour my hue.

I descend from Afrika; I am Afrikan that's me.

Call me what you will, it doesn't impact me,

because I know my legacy, my history and my
descendancy.

Name calling and labelling will not erase my identity.

Because I know I am Afrikan. Afrikan! That's me.

Mama

She was a singer and a dancer too.

A storyteller, poetess, and proverb guru.

Many a moonlit night with the crickets
chirping,

She took us to fantasy land with her story
telling.

She told of the escapades of a brave fairy,

but some of her other tales were scary.

She frequently repeated proverbs to learn,

To better our lives at every turn.

Many of these morals still ring in my ear,

Some of these, with you I'll share.

For delaying homework- *"Leave not till
sunset what could be done at dawn."*

*"Don't let the right hand know what the
left-hand knows,"*

Means, *keep your secrets from friends and foes.*

"Delay is danger."

Warns not to procrastinate,

Things get worse if left for a later date.

"What goes up comes down,"

Means, retributive justice is around.

"Look before you leap,"

Means take care.

And *"Think before you speak,"*

Means beware of what you say.

A stitch in time saves nine. It gets worse with time.

"Forewarned is fore armed,"

Keep your plans to yourself so others don't know what you plan.

Other adages which my mother, regularly did utter:

*"Be as wise as a serpent and harmless as a
dove."*

Means, take time before showing dislike or
love.

"Your tongue is your worse enemy,"

Your words will condemn you and me.

I tried to do the same with my family,

but they take the words literally.

I said to one, 'don't muddy your water!'

He replied, 'where is the mud, mother?'

The new generation understands life
differently,

with a totally new conceptuality.

Does any of these proverbs ring true with
you?

Or, do you think that they are outdated too?

My Son

Faithful and loyal,

Generous, dependable,

Reliable too.

Spring is Coming

It is March 21 and spring is in the air.

Leafless trees are budding, cherry blossoms blooming.

Birds are singing sweetly, and daffodils sway gently.

Blue bells nod beneath the trees,

dandelions smile sweetly in the breeze.

Daisies dot the lawn; a bright new day is born.

The winter months are fading,

though winds are harsh at times,

but we have left that behind.

The sky is blue and clear, the sun warm and bright,

The air is fresh with not a cloud in sight.

Nature is awaking and new life beginning.

Positive vibrations energize the day,

peace and contentment are on the way.

For spring is here today

Winter Solstice

Darkness and gloom fall,

December twenty two brings

Long dark nights for all.

The Fulani Woman

Jet black velvet skin, she was
slender and tall,

this Fulani woman stood by her stall,

just a space between two other traders,

One displaying cola nuts, and the other red peppers.

The Fulani woman wore a colourful wrapper,

around her waist, draped over one shoulder.

Her face was adorned with Henna markings,

and arms were painted with similar drawings.

On her slender feet she wore leather sandals,

covered with Fulani symbols.

Her hair was braided in sleek cornrows,

with cowrie shells in-between those.

She had a low wooden stool on which she sat,

then she twisted a cloth into a mat.

She did not call out what she had to sell,

unlike other traders who shouted or yelled

Bitter leaf! Gari! Egusi! Ewadu! Amala!

What was she marketing? I did not know,

I didn't wait long to discover though,

'cause the first customer came in front of her,

And between her legs on the mat,

the patron comfortably sat.

There was no chit-chat nor discussion,

So I waited to see what next would happen

between the customer and the Fulani woman.

She took a comb from her wrapper,

and nimbly, the customer's hair she unplaited.

And section by section she then parted.

Her fingers worked electronically,

Quick and nimble, in and out mechanically,

while her golden arm bracelets jingled musically

as braid by braid appeared magically.

The hair was all done in half an hour,

and the customer rose and paid her one Naira.

Many heads later, she stood up from her stool,

and twisted the cloth mat into a spool,

placing this on her head, she balanced the stool.

With straight back and stately stance, she walked away.

Would she return another day?

Springtime

Nature is waking,

New life comes into being,

Light, life, and loving.

Zoom

COVID lockdown has not been all doom,

It has saved travel money and introduced Zoom.

Zoom opened closed doors electronically,

And increased our use of virtual technology.

You can join Zoom meetings globally,

or perform to audiences internationally.

You can attend your early lectures while still in your bed,

And you do not have to show your face nor your head.

You could be in your birthday suit in bed.

Even people age 94, handle Zoom successfully,

to contact with their friends and family.

If you like archaeology you can go on a virtual dig,

Or roam in a jungle that is wild and big.

Zoom is lots of fun,

you meet people you don't know.

You can attend live concerts, or a drama show

Zoom saves traffic jams and travel costs too,

but do exercise...

Please, please, do.

Zoom can be lots and lots of fun,

but take breaks in between, before the day is done.

Rise from your computer every thirty minutes,

and walk around to maintain muscle fitness.

Ode to Bob

Just a mongrel dog,

Devoted and steadfast you,

Faithful, loyal too.

Life is for Living

You might retire at a certain age

But please keep engaged.

Live life to its fullest regardless of your age.

Learning is lifelong so keep those brain cells firing,

Learn something new each day, something of your choosing.

Join a workshop or take a course you'd dreamt of doing long ago.

These things will stimulate and increase your knowledge too.

The brain is like a muscle so stop it from retiring,

by learning, visualizing, analyzing, and reading.

These things increase mental agility which can reduce brain senility.

Life is for living,

So live it to its fullest.

Age is just a number so disregard it.

Keep your brain cells working to stop them declining,

Learn a new language, reflect on an old skill that may need fine tuning.

Keep your muscles working, stop them from declining,

Do dancing, gardening, exercising, or walking.

Physical activities are very good for you.

Activate your brain and your muscles too.

Appreciate

Give thanks for each day,

And enjoy every moment,

Live life all the way.

Tickle your Palate

Have you ever cooked or eaten a Nigerian dish?

When I explain, you would wish.

There's pounded yam with Egusi and cod fish,

a very tasty dish.

Amala and Ewadu with mixed meat

Not forgetting the red pepper bringing loads of heat.

There is bush meat, very tasty too,

You may get wild rabbit or deer meat too.

There is gari made from casava,

eaten with bitter leaf soup and a meat palava.

Then there is moi-moi, O how I love this!

It is pounded black eye beans with shrimp and
condiments,

steamed in banana leaves which adds to its flavors.

Jollof rice is very, very nice

This is a mixture of meat, red pepper, palm oil and rice.

The main constituents of Miyam Kuka soup are the leaves of the Baobab tree,

These have micronutrients, vitamins and protein in plenty,

Which helps to keep the immune system strong and healthy.

Ungungo is a favorite dish of mine,

This is steamed goat's head soup with herbs such as thyme.

We start the meal by traditionally breaking cola nuts,

and honor the ancestors with libations,

offering them traditional venerations.

We proceed to wash our hands in gourds,

then eat with our fingers, not with forks.

The food is washed down with fresh palm wine,

harvested from palm trees the morn before we dine.

These meals are delicious, nourishing and tasty,

Join me in a traditional Nigerian delicacy.

Be Thankful

Don't let the sun set,

without giving praise and thanks,

For the day's events.

Tap into them Now

Your elders may have lots to share.

Tap into them now,

'cause when they are gone, they are gone.

They can tell you firsthand how things used to be,

and may share secrets hidden in their memory.

They may give insight in the turns their lives took,

which may not be written in a history book.

You may discover blood lines that you never knew
existed,

or understand the value of relics you overlooked
or missed.

Elders could share words of wisdom, or shine light
on things long forgotten.

They can tell you of the fruit and berries that they
ate,

That are no longer eaten, in this processed food date.

Do not discard your elders,

they're your living ancestors.

Ask them...

What?

When?

Why?

How?

Don't delay, ask them now.

They may tell you things that happened long ago,

or disclose traditions that you do not know.

Many folks are paying for DNA ancestry, so while you can, take the opportunity

to ask about blood lines, from dear old granny.

Documents may sometime lie and lead you astray,

like something I heard the other day.

The name on the birth certificate was not the
mother.

Gran disclosed that the boy

Is the child of the woman he calls godmother.

And the one on the certificate was her boyfriend's
sister.

This resolved the confusion in the DNA ancestry

Which show blood relatives that were a mystery.

Do not leave it long to talk to your gran,

Because when she or he is gone, they are gone.

Youth of today are the elders of tomorrow.

So enrich yourself today for your future.

Nigeria

So varied and vast,

Many customs and cultures,

Languages in mass.

The Widow

Brother-in-law, you are loyal, good, and true,

but you fail to understand that I cannot marry you.

You are my husband's brother and I do not love you.

Your traditions are realistic, but alien to me.

You would not contemplate or even try to see,

that this type of marriage is not for me,

who hails from a different country,

with a different marriage ideology.

You fail to realise that I cannot marry thee

That your marriage proposals are unthinkable to me.

You threaten to take my children if I do not abide by
custom

and accept your ring in a marital union.

You left no stone unturned to enforce your tradition,

disregarding the norms of my own nation.

You refuse to see that I am a strong woman

That fights for my rights with courage and determination.

You left me no choice but to take my progeny

and leave all else behind, in your country.

Many years have passed by, and you are sadly gone,

and departed to the great beyond,

What would have become of me?

If I had wedded thee?

Would I be forced to marry another brother-in-law?

Or a male that I did not know?

Am I difficult?

No not me.

I'm just a determined widow you see.

The Moon

Hail! Large silver globe,

You gently light my pathway,

With rays from your orb.

Ode to Queen Ndate Yalla Mbodj

Brave Ndaté Yalla Mbodj

of Senegambia dynasty,

You've gone down in history

Queen Ndaté Yalla Mbodj

You wore your crown with honour and pride

With the royal staff by your side

On diplomacy and military skills you relied.

Queen Ndaté Yalla Mbodj

With persistence and determination

You fought for your kingdom

To free it from French colonialism

Queen Ndaté Yalla Mbodj

The French took your nation and country,

Not with courage nor bravery,

But with superior weaponry

Queen Ndate Yalla Mbodj

You're a symbol of African liberation,

An icon of Afrikan freedom

Inspiration for the future generation

Queen Ndaté Yalla Mbodj

An emblem of female empowerment

a symbol of gender equality

a beacon for Afrikan humanity.

Queen Ndaté Yalla Mbodj

UN-MASK IT

We are bombarded with fake news and false information

And lots and lots of sensational revelation.

Distorted proclamations are barriers to improvements,

Resulting in wrong or warped responses.

Fake news comes through various venues like TV and radio,

Newspapers, Facebook, WhatsApp and such like media.

But worse, is when this news comes from a significant other,

A friend, family member, or a brother.

Because we tend to believe the things that they utter.

Misinformation can distort our vision of the world's economy

And impact on all of us negatively.

It can damage health, and injure us financially.

Propaganda can cause wars and good things hijack

So never take what you hear as fact,

But allow for it to be given from front to back.

Some folks may tell you what they think you want to hear

Or may twist things to make them sound excitingly clear.

News may be embellished to make it sound real good

Or be scandalized, for your attention to hold.

People may relate things from their own perspective

From their subjective views and not the objective.

Conspiracy theories and false news abound,

especially now that COVID19 is around.

When you read, see, or view items on the internet,

Fake news is what you could get.

Analyze all you read, see, and hear.

Check things out, have no fear.

Peel back the masks and view the contents bare.

Ask, scrutinize, and critically analyze.

Double check to separate fact from fiction,

that may come from the teller's diction.

Peel off the masks, conspiracy theories abound

Fake news and false information are all around.

Ode to Tom

Seventeen years long,

You Tom Cat, stood by my side,

Sadly, you have died.

Queen Ndate Yalla Mbodj
1810-1860

My name is Ndate Yalla Mbodj,

Born in 1810, I'm Queen of Waalo Kingdom,

A Senegambian Empire's nation.

King Amir Fatima was my father

Queen Awo Fatim my mother,

Ndjeumbeut, my sister.

We were trained in weaponry,

Military tactics and diplomacy,

Ancestral customs,

and our sacred religions.

At 16, I wedded King Yerim in political union,

and was widowed at age thirty-one.

Prince Tassé Diop asked to marry me. He's a
commander-in-chief of my army.

Our marriage was blissful and happy.

Sadia, the only child I bore, was cherished and
adored.

He was the love of my life,

Whom I kept from harm and strife,

In 1846 I ascended the Waalo kingdom when the
queen, my sister, had passed on.

I rule with courage and wisdom,

Political skills and intuition.

I developed female warriors,

who were Waalo's protectors.

I defend my family, my kingdom, my people, my country and nation from Arab, Moor, and French invasion.

Using my military prowess.

I challenge the French colonists,

Headed by Loui Fayderbe, an imperialist.

Many a fierce battle I did win

Against the barbaric butcher and his henchmen.

I oppose the French's insatiable demands,

against stealing my lands.

Burning villages and looting farms,

pilfering my best oxen and lambs.

Seducing and raping our young maidens,

Robbing my treasures again and again.

All reasoning and suggestions the French disdain.

They arrived in mighty bands

settling on more and more of my lands.

With my smoking pipe I meditated,

And puffing its sacred smoke, I contemplated.

I'll fight and vanquish the invaders,

and protect Waalo from these marauders.

I'll fight for my kingdom,

and defend my nation.

"Rise up ye warriors, chiefs, and army!

Make ready your weaponry, charge your rifles,
come fight.

Vanquish the French, send them on flight.

Beat war drums. Banish them from Waalo's sight.

Shoot! Shoot! Shoot! Blow them down,

clear them from all around.

Guard and protect our motherland,

fiercely fight for our kingdom."

In 1855, Fayderbe with army and cavalry,

conquered Waalo country,

with their superior weaponry.

Exiling me far from my territory.

Many losses have been my part,

but the French's capture of my son pierces my
heart,

And Waalo's conquest is the poison dart,

That sent me to join ancestors in 1860,

at the early age of just fifty.

Today, Waalo is part of Senegal and Gambia.

In Francophone West Africa,

a statue of Queen Ndate stands in Dagana.

In Senegal which borders Mauritania,

Queen Ndate is a symbol of female
empowerment.

An emblem of African liberation,

a heroine of resistance against French
imperialism.

SUMMER

The time is crazy,

All are buzzing and busy,

Life is not lazy.

Chaos

They came in their hundreds,

They came in their thousands.

They came from all over the land,

to listen to the leader of the band.

Some wore tee shirts

with extremist letterings,

While several held flags with allied wordings.

Many wore stab vests, knee pads or conspiracy hats,

and lots of heads were crowned with red caps.

Some waved banners showing alien symbols,

while others showed off United Boys' logos.

Some had on vests with supremacy insignia

or with phrases such as 'End the Media'.

Several wore balaclavas and camouflage gear,

And appeared as though they were ready for war.

Others looked like tourists going out for the day,

but they all adored this leader in their own special way.

Some carried batons, others held rifles, or sported
baseball bats while others had mobiles.

They went to the government building to listen to the
president

Who loudly broadcasted that the election was fraudulent

He claimed that the votes were stolen

and the country from them is illegally taken.

The mob shouted loudly at this proclamation,

and he looked on them with deep admiration.

He observed these supporters, they were his followers.

With a smile he declared in a measured vocal

'We are going to walk down to the statehouse'.

This is democracy, political citadel.

Provoked and egged on by this announcement,

The mob cheered in wild excitement.

Loud shouts could be heard,

as they listened to their leader's every word.

His fueled rants spurned them forward.

Scuffling, scrambling, and pushing onward,

towards the statehouse they went hurrying,

As though an irresistible force sent them scurrying.

The congress was in joint session,

to ratify the president-elect's coming,

But the riotous bands could not care less,

because they were bent on disrupting this.

They climbed the statehouse' steps with little interruption,

and scaled the walls with ardent determination.

Police retaliated with tear gas and pepper spray.

A miniscule response compared to the minority movement day.

The thugs swarmed the stately hall,

trashing and defacing this majestic cupola.

73

They wandered in the halls of Senate chambers,

searching for journalist and political members.

Some police opened doors for these invaders, while others
posed for selfies with the intruders.

Senators and journalists frightened and shaken,

Fled from this murderous invasion,

they cowered under desks or crouched on the floors.

While the vandals shattered windows and doors,

smashing furniture, destroying and ravishing,

scattering papers, documents, and pilfering.

Chaos in the statehouse laid all around,

and calls for 'gallows and blood' abound,

While the thugs searched and the halls but no victims
were found.

'Hang the VP' could be heard

From some voices in the crowd.

One entered the speaker's office and in her chair reclined,

but thankfully, the speaker, he did not find.

Some of them sported zip-tie hand cuffs.

I shudder to think what they might have done with this
stuff.

Two policemen were seen running for their lives,

As the mobs advanced like angry bees from hives.

Police shields and other things were stolen,

and a fire extinguisher was flung on a policeman,

Causing his life to be ultimately taken.

Thanks to digital technology,

the world has seen the near shattering of democracy,

In the earth's most powerful society.

It was deadly riots, attacks, and commotion; mob violence
and pandemonium,

Six lives were lost, but this could have been worse,

because an arsenal of incendiary devices were found,

Pipe-bombs, pistols and Molotov cocktails were hidden all
around.

Two full days after this riotous cacophony,

the president condemned the insurgency,

but said to the hooligans, 'I love you', despite their
treachery.

Wednesday the 6th of January, will go down in history,

Mr. President, will be remembered as the failed dictator,
autocrat, liar and democratic coup initiator.

For the country, this is a new beginning.

How will it develop and what will be its ending?

A similar thing could happen to us here,

if we fail to learn from what happened over there.

Autumn Leaves

Leaves turn gold and brown,

Some turn to red and yellow,

Others green, year-round.

Catalyst for Change

Born in nineteen seventy-four,

but in May twenty-twenty, he breathed no more.

He was someone's son, someone's brother.

Someone's nephew and someone's father.

A special friend and someone's partner.

This African American man was arrested by four
policemen.

Restrained, handcuffed, pushed to the ground,

and lying prone with his belly down.

A white police officer, knelt on his back,

and with maxim force he placed his left knee
on the man's neck.

The man cried out *I can't breathe* and his nose bled,

but the officer applied more pressure to his neck instead.

The man gasps again, *I can't breathe, I can't breathe,*

my stomach hurts, I hurt all over. With that, he called out for his **mother.**

The officer kept his knee on the man's knee for 8 minutes and 46 seconds,

Until the harbinger of death most surely beckons.

With a glint in his eye and slight grimace on his face,

The officer pressed harder and harder on the man's neck, because of his race.

The man begged for mercy, but more pressure
was applied,

he asked for water, but this was denied.

Eight minutes 46 seconds the officer held his
position,

While his comrades stood by until the man's
expiration.

Finally, the man called out 'Momma, Momma'

To his mother who died but 2 years ago,

while the spark of his extinguished so.

He was taken ultimately, but he has made a
difference.

Out of his death has come national and
international movements,

positive changes and numerous improvements.

His protests instigated a global reassessment of
racism,

Racial harassment, prejudice, and discrimination.

It stimulated international uprising of a
movement,

and sparked a global reassessment for racial
equality and improvement,

like the removal of monuments of colonialism and
slavery.

Down came the statue of an officer of the
confederacy.

Choke holds in the North Star State are banned,
and a statue in a Caribbean island has come down.

While a slave trader's statue in Bristol was pulled
to the ground.

Statues of Spanish explorers were removed in the
North Star State Capitol and Green Town.

July saw the bust of an imperialist, decapitated.

He was a white supremist and an architect of
Apartheid.

And plans are underway to remove his statue
from Oxford town.

The murderous policeman has been convicted of
third-degree murder,

All well as second-degree manslaughter.

He is sentenced to 30 years in jail,

with good behaviour he could be released in ten
without bail.

His defence lawyer blamed the man's death on
him,

but the jurors saw beneath this deception.

The man's death was not in vain.

Many positive changes have been gained.

Rest in peace, my son, your work on earth has just
begun.

Winter

Outside it is cold,

The winds are strong, fierce and bold,

Home is snug and warm.

Have you ever wondered what viruses are?

They are microbes that cannot be seen with the naked
eye

Only with electron microscopes can we, them, espy

They are classed as non-living entities and on others they
rely

Forcing host cells to reproduce them and in millions
multiply

Their hosts are mammals, bacteria, plants, birds, and even
the common fly.

Viruses are abundant and exist far and wide

in air, on land, fresh water and in the ocean tide.

Each and everywhere you'll find them,

in the smallest ecosystem.

There are trillions of viruses

And they come in different shapes and sizes

in arrays of beautiful colours too.

Some are pretty when they come into view.

Some viruses are helpful,

others cause no harm to man.

A few cause diseases like the common cold and flu.

There are many others, I will name a few...

Chicken pox, warts, shingles, cold sores,

Small pox, viral hepatitis, Ebola, HIV and SARS.

Sometimes they cause pandemics like the Spanish Flu

And COVID19 resulting from the virus SARSCOVID2.

The latter is currently upon us

Causing sickness and death and lots and lots of fuss.

Viral diseases are spread in many different ways...

Like respiration, copulation, touch, and ingestion.

They can mutate and change

And attack the drugs targeting their range.

Antibiotics are useless against these microbes

So please don't ask your doctor to prescribe those.

No bomb, drone, nor usual arms will affect them

Only anti-viral drugs and vaccines can control them.

A good immune system will help in the fight

Try to strengthen yours and set it right.

Practice good hygiene in everything you do,

to stop dangerous viruses from attacking you.

Life

Life is for living,

Welcome each day joyfully,

With true thanks giving.

Genocide?

What happened to the Neanderthals that lived in
European land?

They existed the same time period as modern man.

No real explanation is given for their demise.

We know that their brains were bigger than modern
man's, in size.

But they did not seem to use malicious devices

Like modern man with his heinous caprices.

I have a theory about how these people died,

They were murdered by modern man and their lands
occupied.

Why have I come to this solemn conclusion?

Because that is what has happened to many a nation.

Just look at the Tasmanians who flourished long ago,

Europeans erased them from history too.

The Germans in Namibia killed most of the Herero and
Nama people too,

American Indians met their death from blankets with small pox disease,

While Australian Aborigines in numbers, were purposely decreased.

Leopold killed 15 million Africans,

but seldom we hear of these murderous interventions.

GENOCIDE is the name of this game,

that caused the Neanderthals to exist only in name.

THE MIND

Visualization

with deep imagination,

and meditation,

bring realization.

Freedom

You take without permission,

and grab without discretion.

I'm generous, trusting, and giving,

I work hard for my living

But you are bent on pillaging,

you take my best into your possession

like an insatiable obsession.

The more I give, the more you take,

yet little acknowledgement do you make.

You tell the world I've got no history,

that I can't rise from poverty;

while you indoctrinate me with your superiority.

Our biggest diamonds adorn your royal podiums

While Benin bronze heads are displayed in your
museums,

You said Great Zimbabwe was built by foreign hands

and that my ancestors did not build it

That ancient Arabs, Asians, or Europeans constructed
it.

You've tried with might to keep me down

and crush me into the dusky ground.

But I continue to soar and rise

Higher, higher to the skies.

You enslaved my people, millions of them

and tell the world we first enslaved them.

You circulate these creeds

to justify your actions and condone your deeds.

African brothers and sisters unite

and from this mental bondage take flight.

Bring our history to light.

Bring our illustrious past into sight.

You are You

Aches and pains may come,

But you are the same person,

A changing human.

SPARROWS

Two wood doves sleek, smooth and gray

search my garden every day.

They gently coo as if to say, *How do you do today?*

Three magpies nest in the nearby tree

Sometimes they squawk or chatter merrily

While blackbirds warble happily.

Seagulls soar in the cloudy sky,

Making a mewing sound as they soar along.

But no sparrows have I seen

although three years in this abode I've been.

I've seen a robin with breast bright red

perching on a twig just over my head.

But no sparrow have I seen,

in tree, on branch nor on lawn green.

Today, July eleventh, at dawn,

while I sat in my garden enjoying the morn,

Two little brown sparrows flew onto my fence

So I held myself still and tense.

I sat as still as can be, so they would not spot me.

One chirped merrily, while the other preened itself busily.

Eventually they flew away, but seeing them had made my day.

O what a delight this sighting has given my sight.

Did lockdown help to clear their way,

And encourage them to come today?

Please little sparrows, come back another day,

And in my garden make a longer stay.

Age is Just a Number

Lines may mark your brow,

But your soul remains the same,

Enjoy your life now.

All that Glitters is Not Gold

You brought me a delicacy from your hood,

but the smell of the main dish was not very good,

And the taste was not what it should.

The sell by date on the sweet was over a year ago.

Did you forget it in the cupboard a long time ago?

Did you get these things especially for me?

Or were they chosen accidentally?

A Lesson in Listening

Don't always take what people say as fact.

Allow for messages to be given from front to back.

Some folks may tell you what they think you want to hear,

Or twist things to make them sound nice and clear.

News may be embellished to make it sound good,

Or be scandalised for your attention to hold.

People may tell things from their own perspective,

Or from their own subjective views and not the objective.

Listen wisely to all that you hear,

and unpack the contents bare.

Ask, critically scrutinise and analyse,

Double check to separate fact from fiction

that comes from a teller's diction.

Be Mindful

Wisely eat your food,

Masticate it thoroughly,

Digest it slowly.

Little Lamb
(Deceit)

So warm and cuddly, fluffy and white,

Soft, innocent, and bright.

Little lamb will you be the leader and the light?

You are now a beautiful young sheep

Still sparkling bright.

You are the best of my flock

The dearest of the lot

You are different from the rest of the flock.

But under your charms is a heart made of rock.

You have not deceived me as I suspected long ago

That a stain marred and dented your aura so.

That your white cloak was the tapestry that hid a
meaner side.

That side from me you could not hide.

I went along with all your charms and what you said and did

But I had a hunch that underneath these charms a menacing serpent hid.

Now I know my suspicions to be true

It's time for parting between me and you.

Little lamb, so fluffy and white

So innocent and bright

You are the white sheep in the flock

The sheep in wolf's clothing

Goodbye, adieu, this is our parting.

Food is Essence

Nutrients are good,

Protein, fats, carbohydrates

Micronutrients too.

Mr. President

Take detergent! He advises, *'It kills Coronavirus.'*

Heed this advice and you may become a medical statistic.

He said he takes Chloroquine on a daily basis

To keep at bay Coronavirus.

Although medical scientists warn of the part

this drug plays in seriously damaging the heart.

Mr. President went without a facial mask while
he went rallying,

His supporters and fans, they copy him,

as illness and death from Coronavirus were spiraling.

'Stop testing for COVID19', he advises.

It sends up the numbers of this disease.

"Slow the testing down please!"

You are increasing the statistics of this disease.

"99% of coronavirus cases are totally
harmless," he declares;

"And children are immune from COVID19 plagues

Open up schools quickly", he says.

Mr. President recently wore a mask, not because it will
keep him or others from danger,

But because he'd look quite nice, just like the *Lone
Ranger*.

He calls Coronavirus Kungflu and openly blames Chinese
ethnicity.

Covertly inciting racial disharmony,

between non-Chinese and the Chinese American
Community.

He made no remark on police brutality,

or the North Star man's murder by four men of
the constabulary,

Instead, he called the federal troops on the protestors

And labeled protestors of the movement, ***Rioters***.

Mr. President caught the virus but quickly recovered

He said, 'It's a blessing— in 20 years I never felt better.'

Disregarding 237,000 Americans that died from Covid

He cares nothing for the sick nor the departed

The polls are in, the president-elect has won

But Mr. President said the results are a pun

and declares that he is the winner.

He plans to stay in the state house forever.

He sacked his security officer,

Because he contradicted claims of voter frauds

Mr. President overturned the bedrock of democracy

Through his disinformation, lies and hypocrisy

Come 20th January 2021, the president-elect will be
the leader of the American society.

Mr. President, why don't you retire gracefully?

Vital Life Forces

Ventilate and breathe,

Get your sunshine vitamin,

Water! Drink that in.

COVID19 Lockdown

On March 16, 2020,

I started isolating,

to protect myself from Coronavirus cross infection.

This unprecedented lockdown opened doors for me
all around.

I'm busier now than I've been before; doing things
I've not done of yore.

Every day after ablution I meditate, then follow the
daily routine I create

I exercise and deep breathe too.

Tai Chi and Shabashi practices, I regularly do.

Daily I walk 1000 steps or more,

circling around from front to my back door

Or I'll go up and downstairs 35 times, while singing
musical rhymes.

I've scanned my address book and diary

Using social media successfully,

Networked with friends and family,

while reaching out to those who are lonely.

I've invented culinary delights, like orange peel tea
and green banana skin bites.

The weather has been fairly good, so I'm enjoying
things in my hood,

Like seeing the difference between a wasp and a bee

And listening to birds singing in the nearby tree.

My creative juices have been stimulated

and lots more poems I've created.

I've written a short autobiography for the magazine,

People in Harmony.

Three online courses I've completed

And mindfulness I have repeated.

I've learnt to compress a massive file, and change
Microsoft word to a PDF file.

I rediscovered my piano keyboard in its package
undisturbed,

And have started once more

To play a little tune each day.

I've discovered who cares about me,

My son, William, and his family

Who are always there for me.

Mandy, Ruth, Vesna, and Valerie,

who do my shopping faithfully.

Nagina, my adopted daughter who cares about me.

Others bring joy to me, by demonstrating their loyalty.

I adhere to six feet distancing and remain in social isolation.

I don't touch my grandchildren physically,

but bedtime stories I tell them electronically.

I sing and dance with online training,

and Mr. Motivator exercising

My perceptions are more aware, and I smell and breathe fresher air

The rays of the sun are warm on my skin, as victim D in my pelt sinks in.

The sky is clearer now at night, and I see myriads of stars shining bright.

I even saw a shooting star streaked by

In the stillness of the night sky

Numerous clouds are visible during the day

Some whose names I can barely say.

Like cumulonimbus billowing by

And nimbostratus darkening the sky,

noise pollution has disappeared

And nature sounds now can be heard

like the rain drops on my windowpanes

And birds singing sweet restrains.

Social isolation has not been too bad for me, in this shutdown society.

Aim High

Try to reach your goal,

For highest potential aim,

Fly high, that's the game.

Don't Let Barriers Shackle You

Don't let Coronavirus shut down and isolation

cause you depression or frustration.

Use your restricted movements successfully

to network with friends and family.

Connect with those who are on their own

by Skype, WhatsApp, Facebook, or telephone.

Use this lockdown to do the things you like

or those things you'd put out of sight.

Read that book you'd planned on reading long ago,

Do something you'd hoped to do before.

Meditate, exercise, and sing.

Much satisfaction these little things will bring.

Listen to the bird songs coming from the trees,

These things are free and cost no fees.

Create a routine and stick to it

So when life returns to normal you'll easily do it.

Read that book you'd forgotten on the shelf.

Do your hair, put on your makeup, and pamper
yourself.

Dress as if you were going on a special occasion,

A holiday or a vacation.

These things will lift your mood

and give your emotions positive food.

Deep breathing exercises are lots of fun,

and mindfulness you can do.

Enjoy the little things in life

Like grass, flowers, butterflies, bees, and birds too.

Try to learn or do something positive each day.

Be happy, enjoy, and live I say.

Join Global Fusion Music and Art

There are lots of things which you can take part in

Like painting, singing, dancing,

developing your skills in writing

yoga, Taiji, and meditating.

There is something for everyone

From children to the elderly and beyond.

Aim For Perfection

Aim for the sky,

Make your goals achievable,

Set your limits high.

The Dog and the Fox

Dog was indisposed one day so Fox came over for a stay,

He brought no gift or token of concern, showed no empathy

compassion nor even sympathy.

Fox was eager, in offerings to partake

but failed to positively donate, though willingly to take.

Dog carefully watched his friend, and saw a real live fiend.

He scrutinised Fox's remarks and silences,

and saw beneath Fox's glitter and envious tendencies,

Which bubbled out with Fox's utterances.

Instead of praise and congratulation for Dog's achievements

Fox displayed overt malice and jealousies.

He told Dog, 'Stop studying, and concentrate on your life's ending',

But this remark caused Dog to start laughing

Fox told Dog to hang his degrees on his kitchen wall,

but this had no impact on Dog at all.

Dog's lifelong friend had shown another side of him.

He told Fox 'Degrees are open for everyone to take, so why destroy a friendship for envy's sake?'

Dog had made a large donation

in his legacy for Fox's friendship and association,

But Fox's attitude erased this contribution.

Every act, good or bad, has a consequence, and earns recompense.

The law of karma has always shown that one must reap what one has sown.

Cease from making snide remarks or harbouring enviousness,

Jealousies and deceitfulness,

because karma will repay you for what you think, say and do.

Spring Equinox

It is March twenty,

The day and night are equal.

Daylight will lengthen.

The Fall

Five thirty at dawn,

on a pleasant wintry morn,

I tumbled down the stairs in a fall,

jamming my right foot against the wall.

I looked in disbelief

with shock and with grief

to see my knee and hip contorted

as down the stairs my body descended.

The pain was agonising,

so terribly excruciating.

On the last step the fall arrested,

and in shock I sat and rested,

while waves of nausea on me descended

and spiralling dizziness transcended.

Thoughts raced through my head

with photographic speed

Images of my children and my friends

Visions of my late husband and dear parents,

flashed before my inward eye

In the vision I'd espy.

When the shock passed, I summoned a local taxi

And a driver came for me.

He was a young Somali,

who assisted me to casualty.

His name is Yesu.

Yesu, I bless you!

This poem is dedicated to you.

Nurse Webster in casualty,

at the BRI saw me.

She was kind and empathetic,

understanding and sympathetic

Non-judgemental in approach,

accepting and without reproach.

She left no stone unturned to investigate my situation;

To see that I had the right prescription

for my injurious condition.

Nurse Webster, I commend you for all you did and still do.

This poem is also dedicated to you.

My mobility is limited,

the pain is inhibited

with strong medication.

I mobilise with a metal frame, a leg brace and a crutch

I use a wheelchair too, but not very much.

My disability will not trap me

because I'll use my resilience and tenacity

to face this adversity,

and utilize this experience for the betterment of me.

Do Not Bear Grudges

Forgive those that hurt,

Negative thoughts will harm you

Positives help you.

The Past Can Influence Who You Become
(Afrika's Glorious Past)

Children of Afrika have pride in yourselves,

because we are not without histories,

we have rich biographical tapestries.

Our legacy does not begin with the Atlantic Slave
Trade,

When many of our people were captured and
enslaved.

They say, little contributions to the world,

Afrikans have made.

Afrikan history is usually seen through Eurocentric
eyes,

And is mostly obscured and hidden by lies.

Thanks to some scholars and historians,

I can share some of our ancestors' contributions.

Afrika had dynamic social systems,

sustainable technologies and innovations.

Let us look at some of these ancient creations.

Have you heard of Great Zimbabwe?

The largest archaeological settlement in Afrika?

An iconic construction bounded without binder or mortar?

This was created by our African ancestors.

This granite drystone wall with its ionic structures,

Was built between 1500 years AD.

Sadly, it stands in ruins today.

We were taught that Afrikans were devoid of history,

But our past was willfully hidden in obscurity.

People without a past have no meaningful tomorrows,

But knowing your history could enhance your future.

Did you ever hear of the Zulu Empire?

A kingdom that thrived in South Africa.

They were an organized nation,

that vanquished the British invasion.

Did you know that Afrikan ancestors smelted iron and gold in the Kingdom of Mapungubwe?

And artifacts like the golden Rhinoceros were made there?

Have you heard of the Songhai Empire?

A large and mighty empire that existed in West Afrika.

You might have heard of the Great Wall of China,

But did you know that a much bigger wall exists in Afrika?

The Great Wall of Benin, was eight times bigger than that of China,

Spanning 16,000 Kilometres in West Afrika.

Our achievements, architecture and technology were assigned to others,

To people who were not even our relatives nor our brothers.

Our treasures were diverted from our descendants' door,

While our existence was described as useless and poor.

We were told that no Afrikan created these extraordinary inventions,

and that they were made by ancient Arabs or Europeans.

Have you seen the rich Benin bronzes in British Museums?

They were crafted by the hands of ancient Afrikans.

What of the mighty, Fearless Women Warriors of Dahomy kingdom?

That fought against the French invasion.

You have probably heard of the stone circles of the Stonehenge, in England,

But did you know about the Senegambian Stone Circles in West Afrika?

There are more than 1,000 stone circles covering an area of 30,000 square Kilometres.

These are the largest concentration of stone circles in the world, says UNESCO.

Despite the above, few tourists visit these phenomenal innovations,

And little emphasis is placed on these creations.

It befalls us, Afrikan descendants,

To learn about Afrika's ancient history and monuments,

And promote and advertise these illustrious inventions.

Learning who we are and where you came from is fundamental,

in developing a sense of belonging that is vital.

Knowing who you are builds confidence and gives empowerment

which is essential for your development.

Remember, lots are kept hidden from us

So as to stereotype and demean us.

Your Past Influences Your Present

Know your past and learn,

Everyone has histories,

From which we can learn.

Air (O2)

I braced the earth and reach the skies.

I am air! I rise, I rise.

I am a vital part of you

Without me you'd be no longer you.

My vibrations give life and liberty

I'm everywhere around you... yet, me you cannot see.

You gasped for me when from your mother's womb you came

And I endowed you with life-giving breath and energy...

Enhancing your existence and what you became.

I am your vital life force and you depend on me.

I boast of many, many faces,

I kiss your cheeks with gentle embraces

And cool the air on hottest days.

Yet, I vibrate in many ways.

In tempest I am villainous as can be,

sending ravishing winds on all that I can see.

I boast of many, many faces.

I am a cosmic force that is me.

I aim to reach my highest goals and take each day as it unfolds,

For I am strong and brave you see, and what I do depends on me.

I am essential to all things living,

and could be generous and giving.

I fan the air to pollinate plants by areal transporting

And scatter seeds by wind dispersing.

In changed form I give life to corals in sea deep.

And organisms underground that creep

I fan the fires and make them bright; cool the arid air and freshen night

In huge tornadoes I spiral in destruction for all to see.

I'm elusive, because me you cannot see

I may kick up a storm and howl and whistle at dawn,

Yet can be serene and calm later in the morn.

I can secret myself in many places,

and I boast of many, many faces.

I am your vital life force, that's me.

Air is Essential

Life depends on air,

Without air we cannot live.

Light, life, love, and air.

COLOURISM

Only brown, red, or white girls sung in our school choir,

A black woman and man were the school cook and
gardener.

I played as Mark Anthony in Julius Caesar,

Only brown, red, or white girls acted as Mary, baby Jesus'
mother,

A dark skin boy was Judas Iscariot, Jesus' traitor.

All the best roles went to the lightest and the worse to the
darkest,

Like the dark boy who played Caliban in

The Tempest.

From my child's eye I saw nothing wrong,

especially as I was benefitting from it all

and at the time accepted it as norm.

Now I know that the behavior is colourism,

a skin colour stratification,

that is a form of discrimination,

which needs to be vanquished and binned for destruction.

Some parents create animosity between their children,

by favoring the lighter to their darker offspring.

Creating lifelong conflict between the siblings

as is revealed in research findings.

Colourism is often times acted out overtly.

and usually accepted whole heartedly.

It was acted out in my playground,

and normalized in the nursery rhymes that we sung.

Such as: "Brown all around, Red at the head,

White at the right, Black stay back."

Regardless of the shades of our hue,

all children sung that rhyme with joy and gusto,

While hop scotching, maypole dancing, or skipping.

Colourism was birthed by slavery,

When the enslavers had offspring from black enslaved
women.

The light skin progeny was given lighter jobs,

while their dark complexions relatives toiled in the grounds.

Colourism is still practiced today,

We must erase this cancer somehow, some way.

It is present in advertising,

the cosmetic industry and entertaining

and when actors resort to skin lightening

Confront and challenge colourism when you see it,

Ignoring it, condones, validates, and perpetuates it.

Let's demote and vanquish it.

Melanin Rich

Colour is skin deep,

Dark skin stays younger longer

Light wrinkles sooner.

THE WINDRUSH GENERATION AND THE HOSTILE ENVIRONMENT BILL

Let's look back in history

to find the origins of the Windrush mystery.

Three hundred and seventy-six years ago...

Women, children, and men of African origin

were captured and enslaved to work in the Caribbean.

These slaves became British West Indian citizens

Who labored for the British plantocracy in their thousands.

They tilled the earth, fork, spaded and hoed

Harvesting coffee, cocoa, tobacco

and producing sugar which was called *White gold*.

That enriched Britain's economy more than a hundred-fold

Financing her commercial and industrial revolution

While strengthening and expanding her capitalism.

West Indians served in the two great wars

soldiering on with patriotism, pride and deep loyalty

To fight and to die for Britain, their Mother Country.

Now, fast forward, 72 years ago, they were called to
Britain to serve again

To fill job vacancies

created by World War Two

Which many local people deemed undesirable to do.

With no hesitation the migrants came to serve their kind
and country

They came to the motherland that they adored...

A land of hope and bounty.

The ship, *Empire Windrush,* brought the first four hundred
and ninety-two

In the year 1948, Tuesday, June twenty-two.

They filled job vacancies like Public Transport, National
Health Service (*to which I belonged)* and the British rail,

Despite having their social and cultural lives curtailed,

By prejudice, racism, discrimination, hostility and attacks.

Like the 1958 and 1959 assaults in Notting Hill by white
youths on blacks.

And bullied by Teddy boys and barred from private houses
and flats

With signs which read 'No Irish, No dogs, No blacks'

And the 1952 Immigration Act designed to close Britain's
doors

Barring entry to coloureds from her shores.

Plus, an election campaign slogan of 1964

That read 'If you want a NIGGER for a neighbor

VOTE LABOUR'

And Enoch Powell's 'Rivers of Blood' prophesy of 1968,

That hasn't materialized up to today's date.

The Windrush migrants never questioned their residential
state

Because they believed their statues were up to date.

These beliefs were reinforced by the Immigration Act of
1971

That conferred *Indefinite Leave of Stay* to them.

Each and everyone.

The contributions and jobs these loyal citizens maintained

Helped to build a global and modern Britain

Theresa May's 'Hostile Environment Bill' of 2013

Aimed to reduce net migration to tens of thousands, this was the dream.

It made life in Britain difficult for those without correct documentation

And caused many Windrush migrants, hardships beyond expectation

Because some had lost their original passports and/or documentation

And to crown it all, in 2009 by Home Office instruction

Their landing cards and records went to destruction.

This resulted in many of them being declared illegal immigrants

Despite paying their taxes and National Insurances.

Some had their driving licenses revoked

Others were sacked from their jobs and left destitute and broke.

Some were evicted from home and left on the streets to rough sleep and roam.

Bank accounts were frozen, and salaries denied

From these experiences some tragically died

all because of the Hostile Environment Bill

that psychologically maims and sometimes physically kill.

Some Windrush migrants were deported,

Others were denied re-entry to Britain when at the airports they reported.

Some people's pensions were stopped

And others had health care suspended or completely dropped.

Some families were split and separated

Some individuals were incarcerated or repatriated

The traumas of the Hostile Environment Bill are too numerous to mention here

But some include despair, depression, dread and fear

Suffice it to say, some experienced extreme calamity

Deep mental scars and total disharmony.

Thanks to pressure groups the Windrush Scandal is being addressed

By December 2018 more than 3000 Windrush migrants

Had their British Citizenships reinstated.

Windrush experiences are not all doom and gloom

There are lots of successful stories with glitter and boom

But I'll recite these on another occasion

Because it's time for me to leave this podium

But before I go, I ask, *"What will happen next? Now that we have Brexit?"*

The Bill

Always be aware,

Even if you are born here,

Laws may change your stay.

MY WEEKEND IN TIMBERSCOMBE

On a bright and sunny day

On the 30th day of May

My group and I assembled in Exmoor

To work, retreat, explore and to do much more.

This is a tale of some of our exploits

Whilst in Exmoor enjoying its delights.

We stayed at a Duddings Cottage.

Where we shared varieties of food,

Including a delicious potato salad pottage.

Our banquet was very, very good.

Duddings Cottages are in Timberscombe

A picturesque place with flowers in full bloom.

It's near Dunster, in Somerset, on idyllic Exmoor,

A part of which we did explore!

From our cottage we espied

Beautiful, undulating hills and forests far and wide.

The scenery was captivating and much more beside.

Close by, is Dunster village, castle, beach and sea

And many other picturesque sceneries to see.

Whilst in this place of outstanding natural beauty

We took the opportunity to investigate, explore and see.

We enjoyed a game of tennis; bounced on the trampoline

Discussed and networked in Duddings' garden in between.

We conducted out annual AGM with precision

Planned, amend and made many a good decision

Some of us walked in Dunster Park and viewed the castle high

And got our pictures taken by a passerby.

We hiked along a back lane to Dunster beach

On one side were beautiful wild flowers, all in our reach.

There were mallows, dandelions, poppies, evening primroses

Buttercups and daisies

Just to name a few of the colourful posies.

We stopped by to see the steam train passing by

With a toot, toot

And puffs of smoke sailing to the sky.

We waved at the passengers on the train

And they waved back without restrain.

At Dunster beach we sat and chatted;

And shared sweets which we carried,

We watched the waves as they rolled in and out

And looked at children darting all about.

On our way back home,

we asked our way

From a kindly woman who did say

"Go straight ahead, turn left, then take that way."

We followed her directions faithfully

But got lost in the forest most certainly!

Round and round in a circle we went

It seemed like hours in the forest we spent.

There was a treacherous bog that seemed to beckon,

Come! Come!

And say "you've definitely lost your way home."

Finally, we exited the forest with a sigh

But hung our heads with embarrassment as we espy

The kindly lady walking by

To her we explained we had got lost in the woods on Exmoor

And was heading back the way we had come before.

After a hundred yards or so

Tired and weary and foot sore

We heard a honk, honk

And we looked about.

We heard someone call out

'Twas the same lady in her land rover

She'd come to our rescue and beckoned us to come over

She drove us to Dunster Village high street

Where the rest of our group we did meet.

We walked along the cobbled street

Where quaint thatched cottages and curio shops abound

In this exotic, little, village *town*

O what a wonderful and memorable weekend!

What an energising and invigorating time we did spend.

We left Timberscombe

On a bright and sunny afternoon

On the 1st day of June.

Our weekend in Exmoor motivated me

To narrate some of what we did in this poetry

to tell about this place of outstanding natural beauty.

Natural Beauty

Nature has it right,

Hills are green and sun is bright,

Marvel at the sight.

PUT ON YOUR SPECS MY FRIEND

You call me a **Monkey**

Do you need spectacles?

My hair is spiralled into coils

But the monkey's hair is straight as poles

You look at me and shout **Monkey**

Are you that blind?

Monkey's lips are thin and straight

And mine are lush and kissable

You look at me and say **Monkey**

have a closer look

because you do not need a microscope to see

my nose is broad to cool the air

while monkeys are thin with nostrils bare

You call me **Monkey**

Where are your observation skills?

Do you lack visual perceptions?

My ears are small proportionally

while monkey's ears are large.

Posteriorly I'm large and shapely

While monkey's bum is flat and squarely

Monkeys are really very hirsute

Which means they are really hairy.

While I have lots of hair upon my head

my bodily hairs are scanty.

Monkey's eyes are close together

mine are far from each other

Your specs need changing for another

Shave off monkey's hair

his skin is white underneath.

His tool is small beneath.

Put on your specs my friend

think and look before you speak

Then you will surely see

who resembles a monkey.

I'm not saying it is you

But it certainly isn't me.

Think Before You Speak

Point your fingers not

For they may point back at you,

Showing the bad you have got.

When I came to England

At 18, I came to the Mother Land,

The land I learned to love, glorious England!

The country I'd known about all my life,

The land of Oliver Cromwell and Henry the eighth.

The birthplace of Queen Victoria and Shakespeare.

I'd even acted as Mark Anthony in *Julius Caesar*,

And recited English rhymes from my nursery reader.

I performed poems by Robert Southey, and Wordsworth,

And gustily sung traditional British songs with great mirth.

Songs like 'Rule Britannia', and John Peel,

Oooooh, how British I did feel!

Bedtime stories were by Charles Dickens and Enid Blyton.

I was well prepared for my mother land, sweet England.

I'd dreamt of daffodils and visualised snow on my skin.

I was really excited to meet my English kin,

'Things aren't always what they seem to be'

I knew about England; the English knew naught about me.

I was asked if I lived in a tree.

Yes! I replied cheekily,

'When Princess Margaret came to my country, she slept in
the tallest tree.'

The questioner was not at all pleased with me,

And reported that I insulted royalty.

On the bus, people refused to sit beside me,

At first, this made me unhappy.

But eventually, I felt like a princess, sitting separately,

With a spare seat for my shopping, right beside me,

While others crammed into a two-seater,

or stood up and fell when the bus turned a corner.

It was later that people begun to demand,

'WILL YOU MOVE YOUR SHOPPING, SO I COULD SIGHT
DOWN?'

I didn't like this, not one little bit,

Because I had gotten used to being a princess,

And resented putting the shopping on my nice dress.

My mother taught me to finish all my food,

because some children are starving bad.

She said, 'close your fork and knife, when you've finished eating.'

Some folks, were kind, caring, generous and sharing,

Like when I was invited for a meal of Bolognese.

I finished the dish and was about to reminisce

when the host filled my plate with more of the stuff.

I was too polite to tell her I had had enough,

so painfully and slowly I finished that up,

But she filled my plate again, to the top.

Mama said, *to close my fork and knife, to show that I'd finished eating.*

I looked for a knife, but on the table, there was only a fork and a spoon.

And Mama never said to close the fork and spoon.

By now, I was bursting and felt as though I would swoon.

I must have turned green or really looked bad,

Because the host said, 'you look terribly sad'.

I could hardly wait to get home to regurgitate.

And still dislike Bolognese till this date.

Now years later I am happy as can be,

I share good and bad experiences in my poetry.

I have got good friends, a lovely family,

Fairly good health, and a good memory.

Challenge It

Ignoring issues?

Confront, combat, and challenge.

Ignore means condone.

The Child and his Brother

At five months the boy begun to crawl,

The house was made safe to protect him from a fall.

Hazardous things were kept out of his way,

And his siblings were warned of safety risks of the day.

One day the child's senior brother,

removed the plug covers altogether.

This posed serious hazards,

had the child touched these devices.

The brother said he was conducting experimentations,

Was he hoping for a live demonstration?

Possibly, a fatal extermination?

When the child was just one,

the family strolled on the local common.

The child sat comfortably in his pushchair

and was safely strapped and buckled in,

his sister pushed him to begin.

Then the brother took over.

Within a minute the pushchair tumbled over,

and the child flew clean out of the perambulator,

He did not hurt himself but was really scared,

Somehow the seatbelt had automatically got undone,

While in his brother's care.

The child was barely eighteen months.

His brother thirteen years his senior,

was asked to take care of him for one hour.

When the mother returned the child was sobbing,

distressed and continued crying.

The brother said the child was crying

because his mother, he was missing.

When the diaper was changed it was a shock

The child's buttocks were badly scorched,

and marks from the fan heater was imprinted there

While his skin peeled

showing flesh bare.

The brother said he had changed the diaper,

and that the child fell against the fan heater.

He had to be held against the heater for a long time

To sustain a burn such as this kind

which was on the little boy's behind.

The brother never admitted that he burnt his brother.

Why did he do such a cruel thing,

to a baby thirteen years his junior?

How could he conceive such wicked plans;

And carry out those deeds with his very own hands?

Unconditional Love

Love all regardless.

Forgiveness is the answer.

Life will be better.

Make others Happy

Make others happy and you'll be happy too

If you make others happy, cheerful and gay

You will be happy along life's way

Make others happy and you'll be happy too

A nod or a smile doesn't cost a thing

But it could to your siblings, happiness bring

So don't be scarce with a nod or a smile

Because you'll be rewarded for a long while

Don't cheat in games,

nor call each other names.

Show compassion to each other

and be kind to one another

Try to make each other happy

And play well together.

Look out for each other, your sister and your brother.

When you make others happy

You'll be happy too.

Make others happy and you will be happy too,

Be caring, sharing, and generous too;

Because when you make others happy

You'll be happy too.

Start from today, be good, be kind and smile away

And feel how good you feel today.

WEEP NOT

Your loved one is gone?

Gone to the far, far beyond?

No! The soul lives on.

Metamorphosis and Memories

I left Barbados only a few years ago

But it has changed, drastically so.

I fondly remember the yellow sand beaches,

and being caressed by the cooling breezes,

I recall the deep blue sea

and white waves dancing merrily.

I reflect on the bright blue skies,

dotted with cumulous clouds.

There was Pelican Island, not far from the shore,

it stands there no more.

A deep water harbor now stands there,

providing for ships to come right into the bay.

I remember the vendors carrying wares on their heads,

Shouting 'carrots, string beans, ackee.

Who will buy from me?'

My sister and I were very naughty,

we waited till the vender reached the end of the road and
shouted ACKEE!

We hid under the bench when she came back,

calling 'who wants to buy ackee?'

I remember the moonlit nights

when Mama told us fairy tales.

Some of them were captivating

Others really frightening.

I remember the bright stars twinkling in the skies,

When there was little light pollution obscuring the skies,

and soaring by were flashing fireflies,

Showing off their bioluminescent bodies

As they flew between the leaves of trees.

I remember when we sung Latin in church

And how proud I was to be a soloist in the choir.

Mass is now sung in English

Unlike Latin that I so relish.

Dad worked in the Merchant Navy.

He spent a long time at sea

And brought exotic things for me,

like a crocodile skin schoolbag that other children envied.

I remember my first bicycle that Dad bought for me,

It was a beautiful Raleigh, and the envy in my street.

I remember the beautiful doll

That Uncle Cecil brought for me

which was thrown away because I was naught.

I used to collect sweet limes from the hedges.

These citrus fruits were really delicious.

Today's children avoid them, saying that they are
poisonous.

Almond fruit now lay on the ground, no one picks them
up.

No one in the country

No one in the town.

I collected some but was stopped on the way,

by a man who said 'You must be new at this bay.'

Why do you ask? I say.

Says he, 'No one eats those things today.'

Now, hog plums are really very nce,

they are filled with minerals and vitamin C.

I saw many ripe hog plums hanging from a tree.

I knocked at the owner's house to ask for a few,

She said 'Yes, are you feeding pregnant ewe?'

I was too ashamed to say they were for me,

so said 'wee!'

Things in my island have changed a lot

and much knowledge of the past, is lost or forgot.

Things Change

Nothing stays the same,

Metamorphosis, is the name,

Change comes yet again.

The Golden Chain

Mama wore a thick gold chain hanging from her neck.

It was an 18-carat rope chain with which her neck was
decked;

It had a large locket with flowers and leaves engraved.

When it was opened, two faded images emerged

Charles Nathaniel, my grandfather, was on the right

At left, Evelena, my grandmother was in sight.

Mama said my grandfather gave the chain to her when she
was sixteen

She promised to give it to me when I reached eighteen.

I often asked my mother if I could wear it,

but she always answered that I might break or lose it;

And that I should wait till I was eighteen.

My uncle Cecil came from the States when I was sixteen

He was my idol and the brother of my mother.

In my eyes he was the best mother's brother.

He sent us many gifts from the States, not just a few

I had more presents from him than any child I knew.

He sent my first real doll that I loved so much

And the pink coo coo clock that on the wall tick tocked.

The day before my uncle left for USA again

he asked Mama to give him the golden chain.

My heart sunk as I heard this and watched her take it from her neck.

She handed it to my uncle so very quick.

Mama had broken her promise to me,

to give me the chain when I reached eighteen

Instead, she gave it to my uncle when I was just sixteen.

A tear spilt from my eye, and something dropped inside

I went to the bedroom so my sadness I could hide.

I consoled myself by the fact that uncle had done so much for us

And that the chain was a material thing that I might have lost,

And the love and friendship of my uncle was more than the chain would have cost.

Years later, I learned that my uncle had given it to Ellen his daughter

Then somehow it went to Lee her brother.

No one knows of the fate of the beautiful gold chain

Or if the flowers and the leaves on the locket remain.

It certainly wasn't meant for me, nor members of my family.

The chain has taught me not to be attached to an item or thing,

Because attachment can many sorrows bring;

Resist from attaching to a material thing

because when you lose it, sadness it will bring.

That incident taught me that promises can be broken

Even when they're made by a significant person.

Self-Reliance

All humans have faults,

Even a mother defaults,

Rely on yourself.

The Pink Coo Coo Clock

Uncle Cecil sent us a pink coo coo clock

that hung on our drawing room wall

Its pendulum swung to and fro as it tic-tocked

it coo cooed on the hour, that little pink clock

One day my curiosity

Got the better of me

I climbed upon a chair and nearly did fall

As I took the clock from off the drawing room wall

I opened its back, and noted how things were

Then I investigated to find out more

As the screws and wheels came out

The spiral spring flew out

And hit me in the eye

But I did not cry

I examined the clock's contents in wonder

As they laid on the floor asunder

I tried hard to remember

How the clock was put together

Were the wheels and screws near each other?

Was the spring in the middle of the back cover?

I could not recall

Where they were placed at all,

but I put everything inside and screwed it up

I wound the clock, but it didn't tick tock

I wound again, as tight as can be

But all I heard was buzzing like a bee

The clock did not coo nor the pendulum swing,

It seemed like if I had damaged the little pink thing.

No matter what I did, it did not work at all,

So I climbed up again and hung it on the wall.

I waited to see what mama would do

when she discovered that I had damaged coo coo.

She was not happy at all, and I had to face my bedroom wall,

For what seem to a child, a very, very, long while.

Caution

Still waters run deep,

check before you dive or leap,

so good you will reap.

THE POULTRY

Mama kept fowl in her back yard.

These were cocks, hens, and ducks too

They were not kept for pleasure

or status nor leisure,

but for Sunday dinner.

I got to know them all and gave them names.

There was speckled Henny-Penny;

Rhode Island red Jenny;

Mee-me the bantam,

and Birdie too.

The cock was Doodle Do.

He knew his name.

He is facey and arrogant and not at all tame,

But he takes to me,

because I feed him separately.

I scattered bird seeds on the ground,

and the fowl would scramble all around.

I taught Doodle Do to follow me instead,

Where I kept the lion share of feed near a rocky bed.

Doodle Do is red and gold and he is strong and bold.

He rules his harem like a king would do.

Each morning he stretches his neck and crows,

Saying *'co-ca-doo-dle-do! Good morning to you.'*

The hens they had a pattern when eggs they laid,

They'd flap their wings and cackle, as if to say

I've achieved something today.

They'll sit on their eggs about a week later,

and hardly leave their clutter.

When Birdie sat upon her eggs, I'd feed her corn and oat,

I saw her carefully turn each egg from bottom to the top.

I counted the days that she sat upon the nest.

It was one and twenty days she sat upon her eggs and rest.

Then with astonishment I saw her turn an egg and peck,

and out popped a little yellow beak.

I called to my sister to come and see,

but she told mama that I was naughty,

and that I was worrying the poultry.

I did not report another discovery.

Now I know that chickens hatch at twenty-one days

And ducks at twenty-eight.

I feel proud that I have learnt the cycle of the hen

And want to explore much more when

an adult I become.

Deaf?

Both ears blocked today

Could not hear what people say,

Like a silent play.

The Bumble Bee

The big bumble bee

he lived in the sugar apple tree,

In its trunk in a dark round hole,

where he flew in and out in a kind of bee stroll.

Buzzing, he flew back and forth from the pomegranate
tree

Burying his tongue deep in every red flower,

returning later to his sugar apple burrow.

The bumble bee, he lived in a hole in the sugar apple tree

He never visited the tall pawpaw tree.

He was large and black with yellow stripes, and handsome
as can be.

He was my friend, and he didn't scare me.

As I watched him fly from tree to tree

I realise my yard was his territory.

Back and forth from the sugar apple tree,

he fed on the pomegranate tree.

The big bumble bee was very solitary.

I have never seen him with friends or family.

He flew from the pomegranate tree

to the sugar apple tree.

One day from school I rushed out to see my bumble bee

I did not find him in the pomegranate tree,

and there was no buzzing coming from the sugar apple
tree.

I peered in his burrow, this was dark and deep

and I could not see him though I squint and peep.

Then I found him upside down

under the sugar apple tree lying on the ground.

He laid there motionless,

and appeared totally lifeless.

O how I cried when I realised that bumble bee had died

and gone from my side.

I hope his spirit soars in heaven,

for all the joys to me he had given.

REFERENCES

Advice for the Windrush generation on what to do next. (2018, April 20). BBC News. Retrieved June 28, 2021 from https://www.bbc.com/news/uk-43823632

Agerholm, H. (2018, April 22). *Windrush Scandal*. Independent. https://www.independent.co.uk/news/uk/home-news/windrush-man-misses-daughters-wedding-home-office-joseph-bravo-a8316276.html

Cecil Rhodes statue in Cape Town decapitated. (2020, July 20). The Guardian. Retrieved June 28, 2021 from https://www.theguardian.com/world/2020/jul/15/cecil-rhodes-statue-in-cape-town-decapitated-south-africa

Gentleman, A. (2018, January 11). *Woman nearly deported after 50 years*. The Guardian. https://www.theguardian.com/uk-news/2018/jan/11/paulette-wilson-threatened-with-deportation-after-50-years-in-uk-leave-to-remain

Gentleman, A. (2018, May 10). *Windrush man left homeless*. The Guardian. https://www.theguardian.com/uk-news/2018/apr/20/i-thought-i-would-die-windrush-man-left-homeless-after-brain-surgery

Gentleman, A. (2018, May 10). *Windrush victim*. BBC News. https://www.theguardian.com/uk-news/2018/may/10/its-destroyed-my-life-windrush-victim-recognised-as-legal-citizen-after-13-years

Gogarty, C. (2021, May 28). *Felled Colston statue.* Bristol Post. https://www.bristolpost.co.uk/news/bristol-news/felled-colston-statue-go-display-5468076?utm_source=bristol_live_newsletter&utm_campaign=daily_newsletter2&utm_medium=email&p=

Grieving mum of Windrush scandal. (2018, May 1). The Mirror. https://www.mirror.co.uk/news/politics/grieving-mum-says-stress-windrush-12390443

HomeTeam History. (2019, October 22). The Last Queen of Waalo That Resisted French Colonialism. https://m.YouTube.com/watch?v=yE0hMzZcKQM

Jones, R.W. (2018, April 19). *It's not just the Windrush generation.* The Mirror. Retrieved June 28, 2021 from https://www.mirror.co.uk/news/politics/its-not-just-windrush-generation-12393375

Kaul, D. (2020). An overview of Coronaviruses including the SARS-2 coronavirus- Molecular biology, epidemiology and clinical implications. Current Medicine and Practice, March-April 2020, 10:2, 54-64

Kraft, H. (2018, April 20). *Burton man from Windrush generation.* Burton News. Retrieved June 28, 2021 from https://www.staffordshire-live.co.uk/news/burton-news/burton-man-windrush-generation-attempted-1471499

Maddox, D. (2018, April 18). *Windrush generation*
https://www.express.co.uk/news/uk/947706/Windrush
-generation-case-Sonia-Williams
case. Express.

Makela, M.J. (1998). Viruses and Bacteria in the
Etiology of the Common Cold. *Journal of Clinical
Microbiology. 36:2, 539:542.*

Rampage at the Capitol. (2021, February 6). The New
York Times.
https://www.nytimes.com/live/2021/01/06/us/washingt
on-dc-protests

Stickings, T. (2020, November 17). *Barbados
removes statue.* Daily Mail.
https://www.dailymail.co.uk/news/article-
8958275/Barbados-removes-statue-Lord-Nelson-
capital.html

St. John, T.M. (2018, December 18). Types of Human
Viruses. Health Fully.
Williams, O., Houston, D. (2021). Photos smuggled
from Crewe vaccine box plant used to spread anti-vax
propaganda. Cheshire Live. February 18, 2021.

Windrush generation: 'I'm an Englishman'. (2018,
April 19). BBC News. Retrieved June 28, 2021
from https://www.bbc.com/news/uk-43794366

Windrush generation: Who are they and why are they
facing problems? (2020, July 31). BBC News.
Retrieved June 28, 2021
from https://www.bbc.com/news/uk-43782241

Windrush speech. (2018, April 24). Daily Mail. https://www.dailymail.co.uk/wires/pa/article-5651537/Windrush-scandal-cruel-example-unaccountable-state-power.html

Windrush speech. (2018, May 3). *Windrush speech.* Runnymede Trust. Retrieved June 28, 2021 from https://www.runnymedetrust.org/blog/windrush-speech-by-his-excellency-guy-hewitt-barbados-high-comissioner

PERFORMANCES

University of West of England, Black History Month Poetry Slam; Fourth annual Celebration, Bridgwater Together Festival; Bristol University; 2018 Black History Month, Houses of Parliament; SARI AGM, Unitarian Church, Brunswick Road, Bristol.

International Women's Day event, City Hall, Bristol; 2019 Singing Retreat, Wye Valley; 2019 Windrush Day: Past & Present, M Shed, Bristol; Bristol Carnival, Elders, Bristol; St Pauls Homecoming Exhibition, Full Circle Docklands, City Road, Bristol; Ujama Radio, Bristol; Mental Health and Suicide Prevention, Kuumba Centre, Bristol; 2020/21 Zoom Events, Global Fusion Music and Art, Greenwich, London; 2020/21 Music and Poetry events, Tanzanite; Friends of St Pauls Open mic. 2021, Elderly Care, Content Creator. Guest Speaker at Bard of Bradford, Open Mic and poetry event.

PUBLICATIONS

People in Harmony Magazine; Veterans Association of St Thomas and Guys Hospitals magazine; Moonshine Arts Centre National Poetry Magazine; Poetry and Covert Magazine.

Made in the USA
Monee, IL
30 September 2021